Photo Musées Nationaux, Paris, page 45

VERSAILLES
IN COLOUR

PREFACE and TEXTS
by
PIERRE LEMOINE
Chief Curator
of National Muséum of Castle of Versailles

NATIONAL MUSEUM OF THE CHATEAU OF VERSAILLES

OPEN FROM 9 h 45 TO 17 h.
CLOSED MONDAY AND HOLIDAYS

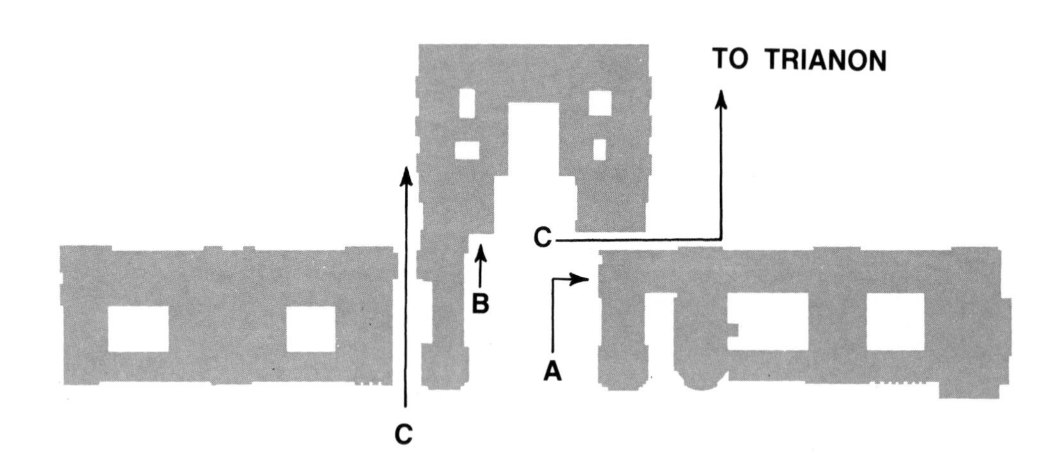

ENTRANCE A

- Chapel
  State Apartments
  Hall of Mirrors
- Museum of the History of France
- Groups having an appointment with a lecturer

ENTRANCE B

- King's Private Apartment (King's Chamber)
- State Apartments and Hall of Mirrors
- Opera House
  Private Apartments

C. To the GARDENS
(Open from sunrise to sunset)

- Visit without a lecturer
- Guided visit conducted by lecturers.
  (Group of 30 persons.)

INTRODUCTION

There is probably no name in France which has as much prestige attached to it as that of Versailles and yet, how many of the millions of visitors who flock there every year see beyond the magnificence of the world's most famous palace and strive to discover its historical significance and deep symbolism? The creation of Versailles can be regarded as the expression of a precise and coherent policy; its decoration heralds the Kings' glory and the efficiency of his government. Versailles may, therefore, be described as being a very accurate image of absolute monarchy.

"A LITTLE CHATEAU MADE OF A PACK OF CARDS"

Yet there was, to begin with, no indication of what its future destiny was to be, considering the modesty of the initial structure and the fact that the estate was, for a long time, nothing but an unpretentious crown dependency until the end of the XVIth century, when it became the property of the powerful Gondi family. From then on it was to have a new destiny.

Henry IV used to enjoy stag hunting in this desolate country of forests and fens and would sometimes go in the company of his elder son; this kind of countryside obviously suited the wild and gloomy temperament of the young Dauphin for later, as Louis XIII, he often hunted here with his select company. Shortly after, he purchased the surrounding land and in 1624 built a small pavilion on a hillock. A few years later, this building was to be replaced by a charming lodge, constructed in brick, stone and slate "a little château made of a pack of cards" as Saint-Simon scornfully called it. Then, having bought the domain of Versailles from the Gondi family, the King enlarged his estate and laid out the first flower beds, turning this charming abode into a sort of hermitage where he intended to retire for the rest of his days as soon as his son came of age.

His untimely death put a stop to these plans but he passed his passion for Versailles onto Louis XIV. The new King went hunting there during his childhood and adolescence. After his marriage, he introduced Queen Marie-Thérèse to it together with the young and brilliant court he had gathered round his person during the first years of his reign. He was soon to undertake the work, that within a quarter of a century, would transform his father's "château of cards" into a fairy tale palace.

He began by renovating the decoration of the apartments and then erected new outbuildings, a small Orangery and a Ménagerie to shelter his ever growing collection of exotic animals.

However, the largest sums were spent on the gardens. André Le Nôtre designed the general layout giving them perspectives that were out of proportion compared with the size of the building. It became evident that the lodge would either have to be destroyed or enlarged in order to put it on the same scale as the gardens.

Nevertheless, for the time being, Versailles was only a "country seat" where the King came to forget the worries and strain of ruling; as can be seen in the Thetis Grotto, Apollo rests, surrounded by nymphs, amidst a scenery of rockery and gushing waters. Louis XIV soon began to come here more frequently and made no secret of his fondness for this new royal house. Moreover, gazettes, engravings and the works of poets soon spread the reputation of Versailles throughout Europe. All that was missing was the consecration of this exquisite abode by great festivities, which took place in May, 1664. The chosen theme, that of "The Pleasures of the Enchanted Island", was taken from Ariosto and is still capable of firing our imagination.

THE NEW CHATEAU

The increasing interest in Versailles soon made it obvious that the Château of Louis XIII needed to be enlarged, so the King resolved to replace it by a larger scale building in order to accommodate visitors for longer periods of time and to make it more in keeping with the monumental proportions of the gardens. According to the original plans, the Lodge was to be destroyed, but the King finally decided to keep it, adding new buildings onto the three sides facing the gardens which thus comprised the New Château. The exact reasons for this decision have never been brought to light; the King may have been reluctant to destroy the lovely house which had been part of his youth, nevertheless, the fact remains that the main parts of the first Château were preserved and their exquisite elegance is still today perceptible in the Marble Courtyard.

The New Château, designed by Louis Le Vau, is totally different from the former one; the façades made of bricks, which blended in gaily with the stone and slate, have disappeared, and so have the high, French-style rooftops. Instead we may now admire a majestic palace in the Roman style with sand coloured façades. These outside walls are animated by statues, low reliefs and protruding columns, the flat roofing being concealed by a balustrade decorated with fire ornaments and trophies. The Italian and distinctly Baroque flavour of the Château is heightened by the presence of a terrace which takes up the centre of the façade on the main floor ("piano nobile").

Two symetrical apartments, each comprising six rooms, are to be found at both ends of this terrace: at the North end the King's apartments; at the South end those of the Queen. They were decorated by some of the best painters and sculptors living in that period; their marble panneling and ceilings decorated with gilded stuccos and paintings are Baroque, the subjects of the paintings taken from antique history and alluding directly to the great moments of the King's reign. The carved and gilded doors, the brocade hangings, the embroidered velvet and the silver chiselled furniture bear witness to craftsmanship far more estimable than the actual materials used. All this, together with the rarest paintings and works of art to be found in the Crown Collections gave these apartments a lavishness unequalled by any other royal residence in France before. A monumental staircase, leading to the royal apartments and decorated with polychrome marbles, sets off the paintings in the vault which are the work of Charles Le Brun and abound in allegories, "trompe-l'œil" and false perspectives.

Meanwhile, Louis XIII's former château had not been neglected; gilded ironwork balconies resting upon pink marble columns, gilded lead ornaments, allegorical statues placed on the edge of the roof had been added to increase its beauty and a slendid gilded gate now separated the Royal Courtyard from a forecourt which is surrounded by the ministers' wings and closed off by another gilded gate. Thus, the part of the palace facing the main entrance came to look as it does now.

A MASTERPIECE OF TOWN PLANNING

Neither were the gardens left unchanged; enormous mounds were created to provide the platform on which the château stands, the ground was moulded fancifully by playing on the different ground levels and clumps of trees were planted to counter-balance the vast perspectives, as well as a multitude of groves. The Grand Canal and the Swiss Pool were dug, then costly channeling works carried out, in order to supply the numerous fountains with gushing water. This is how the designer of these gardens, Le Nôtre, put the finishing touches to this perfect model of a "jardin à la française" and what is also appropriately known as the "jardin de l'intelligence."

By placing a slowly increasing number of bronze and marble statues, the most famous villas of Antiquity seem to be called back to life under the dappled sky of the Ile-de-France. The iconographical theme of these statues mostly comes from the Legend of Apollo and they probably make up the most important series of sculptures in the round executed in France. For this reason, Versailles can be considered as being the most extraordinary open air museum imaginable. Once again, it was Le Brun who provided the designs and ideas that the sculpters were to translate into marble and bronze.

Meanwhile, a whole town was in the process of being built. Its plan spreads out harmoniously from the main axe of the château for fourteen kilometers. The town, château, gardens and park represent, from that time on, the most grandiose example of town planning and served as models for all modern capital cities. It was also at that time that the Champs-Elysées, a rival project in urbanism, were being built.

"A KIND OF REGAL BEAUTY UNIQUE IN THE WORLD"

In 1678, when the Treaty of Nimègue sanctioned the supremacy of Louis XIV over Europe and when his reign reached its zenith, the palace seemed to be on the point of completion. And yet, hardly had peace been signed than the King undertook new projects. The resources, previously used for war purposes, were now devoted to his favourite château. Under the guidance of a new architect, Jules Hardouin-Mansart, Versailles became the grandiose edifice which we know today.

It was at this time that two long South and North wings, destined to house the princes and the courtiers were built, together with the Grand Stables for saddle horses; the Small Stables for the carriage horses and the Grand Commun, which was the living quarters of the servants and where the kitchens were to be found. A new Orangery was built at the same time; an imposing edifice which, with its two vast staircases, formed a cyclopean base to the long horizontal perspective of the château.

However, the main creation of this period was the construction of the Grand Gallery, built where the terrace used to be on the first floor. The most precious materials were used for this gallery which gloriously marks the end of the Grand Apartments; rare marbles, gilded bronze and the mirrors, above all, dazzled contemporaries by their size and number. Indeed, mirrors of this size were a great novelty, rendered priceless by their rarity; the decoration of this vast gallery and its two salons, almost exclusively with mirrors, bears witness to unparalleled magnificence.

Le Brun was responsible for the painting of the vault and he excelled himself by producing a masterpiece which was to serve as a model for regal decoration. These paintings glorify the King and depict the achievements of the first part of the reign, from the beginning of his personal government to the Treaty of Nimègue. Thus, in the principal hall of the château, the deeds accomplished by Louis XIV in less than twenty years have been emphasized. No other decoration could have better fitted the château which was henceforth to witness the splendour of the monarchy for a hundred years. Madame de Sévigné's phrase is fully justified: "It is a kind of regal beauty unique in the world."

The Château became a vast and pagan poem, but one essential element was missing: a monument to recall the fact that the master was not only a mythological hero but also a King of Christendom. For a long time, a temporary chapel was used, awaiting the triumphal church which was to crown this work of art. The final Chapel, begun in 1699, was not finished until 1710, five years before the death of Louis XIV.

The Royal Chapel is a majestic building in white stone and respects the tradition of two-floored palatine churches. Its delicate proportions and elegant colonnade give it a noble aspect; the gold of the main altar and the organ gently glitters in the light which pours in through the high windows. Sculptures of a rare finesse decorate the walls and admirable low-reliefs illustrate the Stations of the Cross. The paintings in the vault, an exaltation of the glory of the Holy Trinity, are a Christian reply to the pagan apotheosis of the King, painted twenty-five years earlier by Le Brun on the vault of the Hall of Mirrors.

The Château had, at last, a chapel worthy of the religious pomp of the French Court. In a building, where architecture and decoration are but the triumphant affirmation of faith, the mighty chords of the organ produced by François Couperin mingled with the majestic sounds of the motets accompanied by choirs and music by Lulli, Charpentier and Delalande.

VERSAILLES, CAPITAL OF FRANCE

However, the King did not wait for these gigantic works to be completed to carry out his cherished project; from May 16, 1682, the seat of his Court and Government was officially transferred to Versailles, henceforth his principal residence and the veritable capital of his Kingdom.

Much has been said about this extraordinary decision which broke with the ancient privilege of Paris. Some maintain that the King was not fond of Paris, having bitter memories of the humiliation he had been subjected to during his childhood at the time of the Fronde. His relative indifference to the Louvre, the construction of which seemed to be never ending, must also be remembered. At the Louvre, he felt he was surrounded by what was still a medieval town. Moreover, the works carried out by his predecessors prevented him from creating a decorative setting bearing the seal of his reign. The fact that he loved the countryside and had a liking for physical exercise must also be born in mind.

At Versailles, which he could justly claim as his personal creation, he had the possibility to erect the château of his dreams and to give himself the arrogant pleasure of modelling nature. By its very size and distance from Paris, his favourite château became a veritable instrument of government as it provided a shelter for the monarchy from the caprice of the parisian mob and enabled the King, not only to gather around his person, ministers, officials and administrators, thus accentuating its centralisation, but also restrained the rebellious nobility by maintaining it in a condition of forced and domesticated leisure. Certainly, the monarchy was to pay dearly for this divorce from Paris, but one cannot help thinking that Louis XIV, by creating a political and administrative capital distinct from the traditional metropolis, anticipated our very age by setting an example which was to be followed later in Washington, Ottawa and Brasilia.

Meanwhile, however, the renown of Versailles had spread far afield. Both Frenchmen and foreigners flocked to admire the most magnificent royal Château and to be enraptured by the spectacle of the most brilliant and refined Court. Allowed to wander around the apartments freely, they were able to be acquainted with the artistic treasures of the Royal Collection and judge for themselves the excellence of French manufactures.

It must not be forgotten that Versailles played a leading rôle in the economic policy of Louis XIV and of his Minister, Colbert. In 1661, the young King took charge of the government at a time when France was dependent on foreign countries, particularly Italy, for all luxury products such as marble, mirrors, velvet and lace. These "foreign currency payments" weakened the Treasury. In order to put a stop to this outflow and to attract foreign customers, the King and his Minister reorganized the ancient Royal Manufactures and commissioned the best foreign scientists, artists and craftsmen to work for them in France. In the Pyrénées, they reopened the marble quarries which had not been exploited since the fall of the Roman Empire. Open to all, Versailles then became a sort of permanent exhibition of French arts and craftsmanship. An Italian, Primo Visconti wrote soon after: "All that is best in the whole world is now made in France."

The outcome of this protectionist policy was beyond expectations; in less than twenty years, France became the leading manufacturer and exporter of luxury products in Europe. The expansion of French art throughout Europe and the extraordinary economic prosperity known in France during the XVIIIth Century originated in Versailles.

Thus, the King was the centre from which everything radiated from and converged onto. Versailles was the dazzling symbol of this sovereign order and erudites took pleasure in recognizing this in the decoration of the Château and Gardens, entirely placed under the sign of Apollo. Louis XIV did in fact choose himself the sun as an emblem and explained why he did so: "The Sun, by its brilliance and the blessings it radiates, is the most perfect image of the King" and, in a way, "... it represents the duties of a prince and prompts me to fulfill them forever."

DAILY LIFE AT THE COURT

In this Château forever being refashioned, court life was organized arounds the different events which made up the King's day. The rigid application of this timetable was rarely disturbed and then only by exceptional ceremonies.

Apart from the time he devoted to his various councils and private conversations with each Secretary of State (which meant eight or ten hours a day), the life of Louis XIV can be truly said to have been public; each subject was supposed to be able to see him go by on his way to mass and to approach him, hand him a petition or be present when he supped. As already mentioned, Versailles was freely open to everyone, even to the most humble subjects, provided they were decently dressed and refrained from begging in the salons. This liberalism, which implied a certain amount of disorder, may seem surprising, but all contemporary witnesses confirm it and such liberalism is in accordance with the secular tradition of French monarchy. This tradition was to be preserved until the end of the Ancien Régime and as Restif de La Bretonne was to write: "Everyone in France considered the King as a personal acquaintance."

In this vast Château of Versailles, the King's inner apartment was his only haven; here he would stay before he officially rose (his "lever") and retired for the night, (his "coucher"), feeding his dogs or spending time on his passion for collections. Nobody was allowed there, except for his closest relations and a privileged few, mostly art lovers like himself. These rooms were the shrine where his most precious collections were kept: famous paintings, such as the "Mona Lisa" and the "Concert Champêtre," gems, precious stones and gold medallions.

As for the Grand Apartment, it was most of the time used as a hallway except for Mondays, Wednesdays and Thursdays, from six o'clock to ten o'clock in the evening, when only courtiers were admitted. Each room was then assigned to a different purpose: one to spread out the buffet, set with vases of gold and silver and ewers, another was used for the light meal which was presented on silver trays and baskets. The third was used as a billiard room and we know that Louis XIV was a master at this game. The remaining rooms were for games, music and dancing. During those four hours, Etiquette became less formal and the King was no longer the sovereign to whom nobody dared speak but the master of the house who moved among his guests, seeing to their comfort and amusement. The most illustrious representatives of every field in France gathered here; the Grand Condé rubbed shoulders with Racine and Bossuet. Speaking of these evenings, Madame de Maintenon reminisced about "the delights of Versailles" and Madame de Sévigné, who was an "habituée", never tried to hide her admiration.

TRIANON

This life of constantly being on display may have seemed tedious even to as tireless a man as Louis XIV, so Trianon was built to provide a haven and also perhaps to recapture the intimate atmosphere of the Versailles he had known during his youth.

The name comes from a hamlet the King had bought and demolished in 1661 in order to enlarge his park. In 1670, Le Vau built on this site, within a few months, the "porcelain house for partaking of refreshments" as Saint-Simon called it. Félibien writes that "this palace was considered as something enchanting because it was built between the end of winter and the beginning of spring and seemed to have sprung out of the ground like the flowers in the garden."

This charming building bears witness to the fascination of the time for everything coming from China; the shape of its roof, the white and blue earthenware tiles that cover the walls, the equally white and blue stucco decoration of its apartments, which all evoke some distant and fabulous pagoda.

Unfortunately, this wonderful little building could not stand up to the winter frost which split the tiles, besides, as the King grew older, he no longer continued to have the same taste for the baroque fantasies of his youth. Therefore, the Porcelain Trianon was to be short lived and was replaced in 1687 by "the little marble and porphyry palace with delightful gardens" described by Saint-Simon and that we can still admire today.

The light comes pouring in through the windows of this one storey building and a "peristyle" (the term comes from Louis XIV himself), links the two main buildings, without interrupting the line of perspective. The pilasters of Languedoc marble standing out againt delicately carved white stone go to make up what really is dreamlike architecture. Inside, the eye is enhanced by the elegance and distinction of the decoration; wood panelling with sculptured flowers, paintings representing mythological scenes, taken from Ovid's Métamorphoses. This inside decoration is an artistic extension of the gardens as this charming abode has only one luxury, that of flowers: orange trees planted in the open, bowers of jasmine and beautifully arrayed flower beds—their colour combinations and fragrances were, moreover, renewed every day.

The King would readily go to Trianon to spend the evening with the royal family and the Princesses' maids of honour. He would sometimes spend the night there or even two or three days without, however, interrupting his ministerial work. It was from Trianon that the King left to die at Versailles, with a serenity and a majesty which commanded the respect of even his enemies.

"LA DOUCEUR DE VIVRE"

Louis XV did all he could to complete the works left unfinished by his great grandfather, above all the Hercules Salon where the marble decoration and vault paintings are in the same tradition as those in the Grand Apartments. They offer the most sumptuous setting imaginable for Veronese's painting, "Christ in the House of Simon the Pharisee."

However, the charms of social life, to be found at that time in the Parisian "salons", were soon attracted to Versailles. The King, who was shy and reserved enjoyed the company of a small circle of good friends and used to invite them to his private "Small Apartments." He also carried out a personal foreign policy distinct from his official one and took refuge in the back rooms with those counsellors who shared the "King's secret." This accounts for the fact that the dining rooms and game rooms are to be found on one side, while the libraries and writing rooms are on the other. Gabriel and Verbeckt were responsible for the painted and gilded wood panelling of these private rooms which the delicate art of the XVIIIth Century was to endow with its most exquisite works. The best painters and cabinet makers contributed to this decoration; silks from Lyons, China from Sèvres, tapisseries from the Savonnerie and flowers from the Trianon went to make up the exceptional elegance that surrounded the King.

On her side, the Queen had her own company and everyone gathered in her private apartments, which had been furnished under her direction in the most delicate taste. Marie Leczinska, attractive and witty, was devotedly attached to her friends and had a sincere liking for fine arts. Though her circle was considered less brilliant than Louis XV's, it was frequented by some of the most highly appreciated wits of the Parisian salons. As for the Dauphin, the Dauphiness and Mesdames, they all lived in great intimacy and often played chamber music together. Thus the unity, that Louis XIV had maintained with authority in his Court until his death, was broken under his successor's reign. The Court became a number of individual courts, existing side by side where the members ignored each other and envied each other's existence.

This lost unity could, however, be reached again on grand occasions, particularly when there were princely marriages and the King had the opportunity of showing off a magnificence worthy of his great grandfather. It was precisely when his grandson's marriage with the Archduchess Marie-Antoinette took place on May 16, 1770, that Louis XV's most important creation at Versailles, the Royal Opera, was inaugurated.

The Court was filled with admiration for the unusually large proportions of the stage, the complex machinery and, above all, the beauty of the auditorium. The new and daring conception of its plan, the perfect proportions, the exquisite harmony of decoration where green and pink imitation marbles blend in perfectly with the blue silks, the gilded low reliefs and the paintings in the vault make this the most slendid auditorium that has been built before or since.

A few years prior to this, Louis XV had had a new part added to Trianon. It is well known that the King had a passion for botany and that he took a great interest in the Jardin des Plantes (botanical gardens), which he created at Trianon, and in Jussieu's scientific research, carried out there. In order to be able to spend more time among the flowers and exotic plants, he asked Gabriel to undertake the construction of the pavillon that is now known as "Petit" Trianon. The perfect proportions of this edifice make it a masterpiece of neo-classical architecture.

If Louis XV and Marie Leczinska knew, to a certain extent, how to preserve the tradition of majestic grandeur that had been the work of Louis XIV, their successors let everything deteriorate little by little; the King through shyness and the Queen through carelessness.

Louis XVI took on conscientiously but with little enthusiasm, this "profession of king" that Louis XIV found so delightful. As for his leisure time, it was divided up between hunting, manual work and reading. For this purpose, he installed several workshops in the attics and increased the number of libraries, the most beautiful one was created as soon as he came to the throne and is revealing of this modest king's studious character.

More noteworthy are the transformations ordered by the Queen; she enlarged her apartments, and gave them a new decoration, inspired from the art of Pompei and Herculaneum. Nevertheless, she left a more vivid memory of herself at Petit Trianon; instead of Louis XV's botanical gardens, she had a picturesque garden designed in the fashion of the day, completed with "fabriques" (little huts), a theatre, where she and her friends acted comedies and a hamlet which, far from resembling an operetta scenery, was a veritable agricultural unit. At Trianon, where she established the customs of château life, Marie-Antoinette tried to forget that she was a queen and cherished the illusion that she lived as an ordinary individual.

Thus passed the last years of the Ancien Régime; Talleyrand was to write of this period: "Those who have not lived before 1789 do not know what is meant by the 'douceur de vivre' (sweetness of living)."

The revolutionary days of October 1789 put a brutal stop to this idyllic like by ringing the death knell of absolute monarchy. The Versailles which had been its sanctuary became its shroud and the wonderful things which represented the work of over a century found their way into museums or were disposed of at public auctions.

Napoléon, Louis XVIII and Charles X all dreamt of restoring the seat of the Court and Government to Versailles. The death of one and the fall of the other two put an end to this ambition. Louis-Philippe realised that a constitutional monarch could not live under the shadow of a king like Louis XIV, so he wisely decided to renounce Versailles as a royal residence. In order to preserve it from ruin and dishonour, but at the expense of some irreparable demolitions, he turned it into a historical museum dedicated to the glories of France.

Thanks to patient work of restoration, the Château has been, for some years now in the process of retrieving its former splendour. Ruined decorations have been repaired, some furniture has found its way back, lost fabrics have been rewoven. Thus, Versailles which has been envied and imitated by all the crowned heads of Europe, is slowly becoming again what it should never have ceased to be; the perfect example of an ideal palace and the radiant symbol of a civilisation.

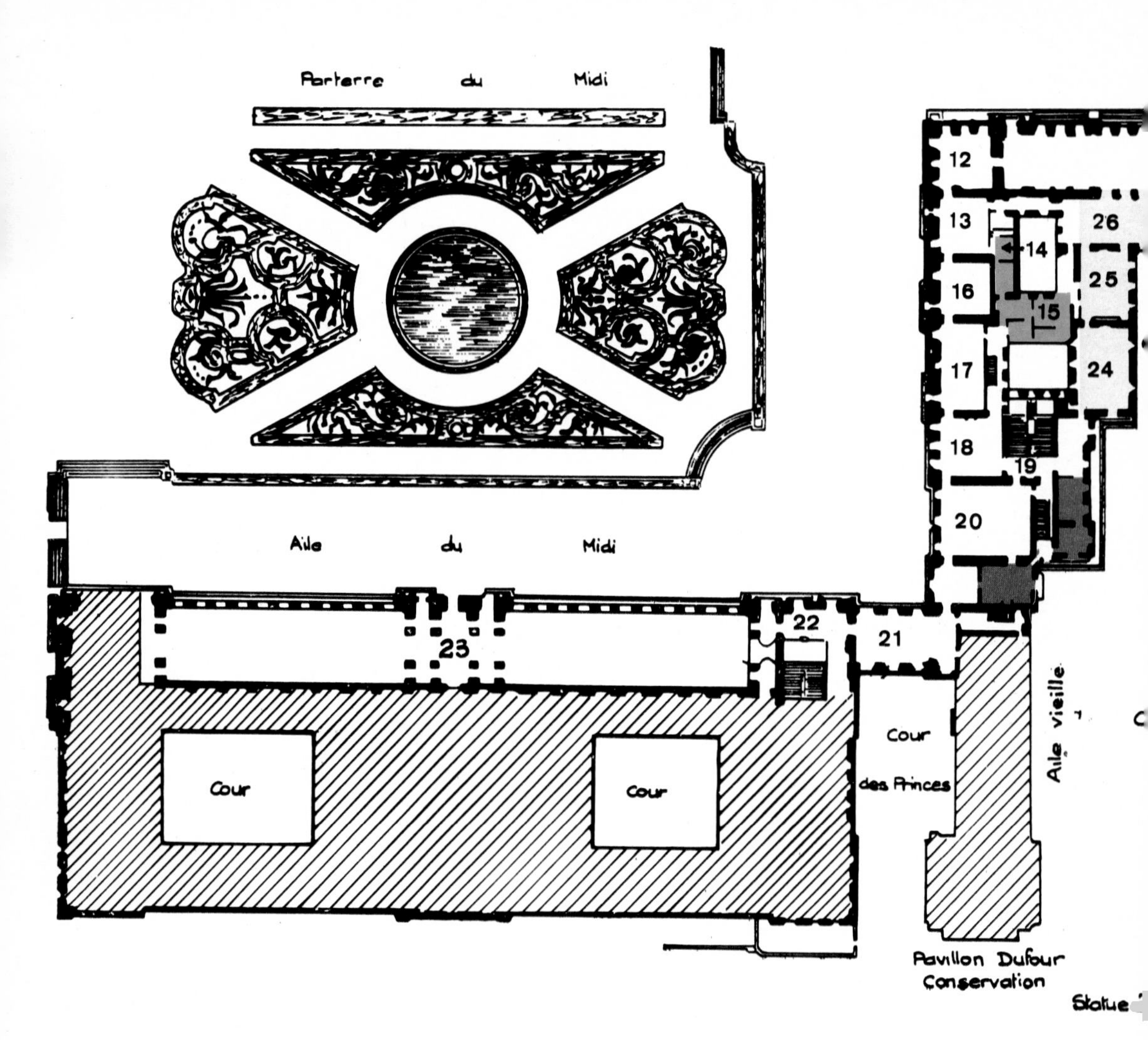

VERSAILLES

1 - The Royal Chapel
2 - The Chapel Drawing Room
3 - The Hercules Drawing Room
4 - The Cornucopia Drawing Room
5 - The Venus Drawing Room
6 - The Diana Drawing Room
7 - The Mars Drawing Room
8 - The Mercury Drawing Room
9 - The Apollo Drawing Room
10 - The War Drawing Room
11 - The Hall of Mirrors
12 - The Peace Drawing Room
13 - The Queen's Bedchamber
14 - The Sofa Chamber
15 - The Queen's Privy Chamber
16 - The Drawing Room of the Nobles
17 - The Queen's Antechamber
18 - The Queen's Guard Room
19 - The Coronation Room
20 - The 1792 Drawing Room

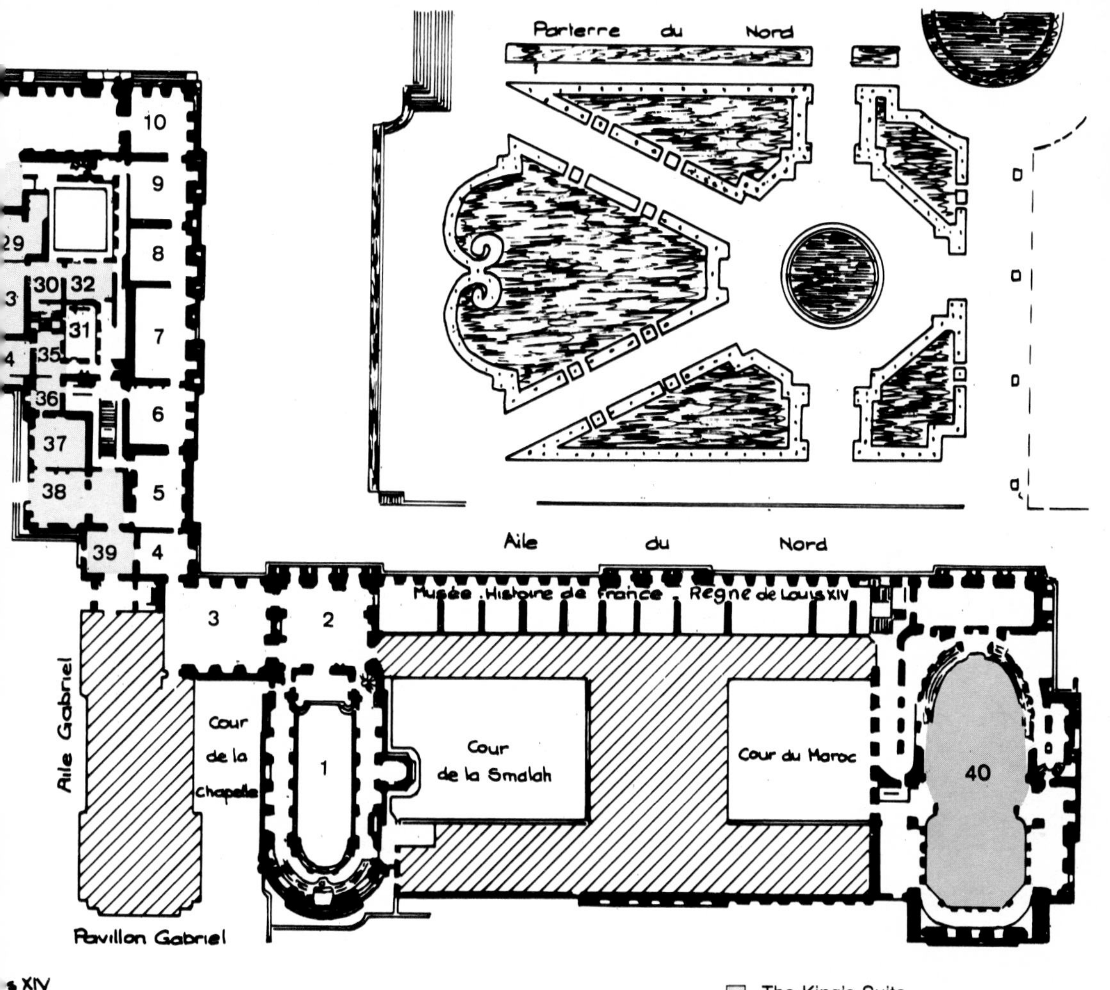

s XIV

THE FIRST FLOOR LAYOUT

- The King's Suite
- The Royal Opera
- The Queen's Privy Chamber
- The Apartment of Madame de Maintenon (Guided Tours)

State Apartment and Hall of Mirrors
Visit at liberty)

21 - The Princes' Staircase
22 - The Battle Gallery
23 - The Queen's Staircase
24 - The King's Guard Room
25 - Banqueting Hall Antechamber
26 - The Bull's Eye window Drawing Room
27 - The King's Bedchamber
28 - The Council Chamber
29 - The King's Privy Chamber
30 - The Dog Chamber
31 - The King's Steps
32 - The Dining Room
33 - The Clock Chamber
34 - The King's study
35 - The Rear Chamber
36 - Room of the King's Gold Plates
37 - The Louis XVI Library
38 - The China Drawing Room
39 - The Louis XVI Game Room
40 - The Royal Opera

THE PALACE

THE ROYAL CHAPEL (1)

This wonderful structure is the fifth chapel of the castle, the first four having only been temporary ones; begun by Jules Hardouin-Mansart in 1699, it was completed by Robert de Cotte and consecrated on June 5, 1710.

Its elegant proportions and its rich decoration make it a perfect jewel, a symphony in white and gold delicately enhanced by the multi-colored marble paving and the vault paintings. These picture the three persons of the Holy Trinity: in the centre "God the Father in all his Glory", by Antoine Coypel; above the royal gallery, "The Holy Ghost Descending on the Apostles" by Jean Jouvenet; above the choir, "Christ Ascending", by Charles de La Fosse; between the high windows are the Prophets foreshadowing the Apostles who appear on the ceilings of the side galleries.

The parallel between the Old and the New Testament is also depicted in decorative sculptures of remarkable quality: at the High Altar with its chased bronzes by Corneille Van Cleve; on the organ-chest decorated by Le Goupil and Dugoulon; on the choir wall entrusted to Nicolas Coustou; along the side arcades and aisles where the foremost artists of the time were called upon.

Following the tradition of Palatine chapels, the Royal Chapel is two stories high: the galleries on a level with the State Suite, where the King, the royal family and the princes of the royal blood were seated and the ground floor where the rest of the court and the public were admitted.

The King attented Mass every day while musicians and singers gathered around the Cliquot organ and executed great anthems with solos, choir and orchestra.

The Royal Chapel was the setting for all the religious ceremonies of the French Court: Te Deum, Order of the Holy Spirit ceremonies, baptisms and weddings such as the one on May 16, 1770 which united the Dauphin (the future Louis XVI), and the Archduchess Marie-Antoinette.

The Hall leading to the Chapel is embellished by a handsome bas-relief showing "The Crossing of the Rhine"; commissioned by Louis XV from the Coustou brothers to replace the Coysevox sculpture which decorates the mantelpiece of the War Drawing Room (see p. 20), it was not placed here until the reign of Louis-Philippe. To the right of this bas-relief opens a gallery leading to the Royal Opera, which, with the upper floor gallery, once served the apartments of the Princes of the royal blood. Today those apartments form the rooms of the Museum of the History of France devoted to the reigns of Louis XIII and Louis XIV; when they are closed we can go directly to the Chapel Drawing Room.

THE CHAPEL DRAWING ROOM (2)

The Corinthian columns and the figures of the Virtues along the arcades blend with those of the Chapel. In the corners of the ceiling, medallions represent

THE ROYAL CHAPEL

the Four continents of the World, and the recesses contain two statues; "Magnanimity" by J. Bousseau, and "The Glory of Louis XV" by Vassé. A large door (marvelously carved) with a remarkable lock opens onto the Royal Gallery where the King, the Queen, and the Royal Family would stand on the beautiful Savonnerie carpet, while the Princes of the royal blood took their places along the side galleries.

THE STATE APARTMENT

THE HERCULES DRAWING ROOM (3)

The vast Drawing Room, standing on the site where the fourth chapel used to be, was begun in 1712 and completed in 1736. The decor of marble and gilded bronze prefigures the state suit and provides a sumptuous setting for two paintings by Veronese: "Eliazar and Rebecca" above the magnificent mantle piece and facing "The Supper at the House of Simon," offered to Louis XIV by the Republic of Venice. It did in fact blend with the colours of the ceiling decor in which François Le Moyne painted "The Apotheosis of Hercules."

The Hercules Drawing Room was the setting for some of the most brilliant court festivities: suppers, balls and receptions for ambassodors.

THE CORNUCOPIA DRAWING ROOM (4)

It was used as an entry-hall to the famous "Rare Objects Cabinet" where Louis XIV housed his collection of medals, now kept at the Bibliotheque Nationale, and the most precious of his jewels, now exhibited at the Louvre. The medals were kept in twelve medal cabinets similar to those seen here: the jewels were depicted by René-Antoine Houasse at the base of the ceiling, in the centre of which he painted the Royal Splendour.

The bronze busts are from the royal collections. Portraits of Philippe V, the Great Dauphin and the Duke of Burgundy by Rigaud, and of Louis XV by Jean-Baptiste Van Loo.

On evenings when guests were received, il was here that buffets were set up on which silver pitchers containing beverages—coffee, chocolate, liqueurs and fruit juices—were placed.

The adjoining rooms were inhabited by Louis XIV from 1673 until 1684. The King then moved to the rooms overlooking the Marble Court (see p. 22), and these rooms became a simple corridor, freely open to all, but on certain evenings they were set aside for the entertainments offered by the King to the courtiers (see p. 10).

THE HERCULES DRAWING ROOM ▲ THE VENUS DRAWING ROOM ▼

THE VENUS DRAWING ROOM (5)

This room and the next used to lead to the State Suite; the doors at the far end opening onto the sumptuous Ambassadors' Stairway which was destroyed under Louis XV. The ceiling, painted by Houasse represents "Venus subdueing the Gods and the Powers," and the voussoirs "Augustus Presiding over the Circus Game," "Nebuchadnezzar and Semiramis Building the Gardens of Babylon," "Alexander Marrying Roxanna," and "Cyrus Taking up Arms to Defend a Princess;" in the corners are the famous couples of Antiquity: "Titus and Berenice," "Anthony and Cleopatra," "Jason and Medea," "Bacchus and Ariadne." Jacques Rousseau did the "trompe-l'œil" paintings: palace views and, between the windows, statues of Meleager and Atalanta. In the recess is a statue of Louis XIV in Roman dress by Jean Warin. Antique busts.

On reception evenings a light supper was served in the Venus Drawing Room in silver filigree baskets.

THE DIANA DRAWING ROOM (6)

This was the billiard room. The ceiling pictures "Diana Presiding over the Hunt and the Sea" by Gabriel Blanchard, and the archings show "Jason and the Argonauts" and "Alexander Hunting the Lion" by Charles de La Fosse; "Cyrus Hunting the Boar" and "Julius Ceasar Sending a Roman Colony to Carthage" by Claude Audran. Above the fire-place is "The Sacrifice of Iphigenia" by La Fosse, and, opposite, "Endymion Sleeping" by Blanchard. At the far end, a remarkable bust of Louis XIV, at the age of 27, by Lorenzo Bernini. Eight antique busts.

THE MARS DRAWING ROOM (7)

The martial decoration of this room recalls the fact fhat at one time it was the King's Guard Room before it was used for concerts and games. The ceiling shows "Mars in his Chariot" by Houasse surrounded by "Victory Upheld by Hercules" by Jean Jouvenet and "Terror Driving off Fear and Pallor" by Houasse. The war trophies in the corners and the wonderful "trompe-l'œil" bas-reliefs recall French victories and the reorganization of the army.

Over the mantlepiece "King David" by Domenichino; to the left "The Family of Darius" by Charles Le Brun, to the right, "The Pilgrims of Emmaüs" copied from Veronese. Portraits of Louis XV and Queen Marie Leczinska by Carle Van Loo. Above the door, four allegories by Simon Vouet.

THE MERCURY DRAWING ROOM (8)

At first an antechamber then a State Room; it was used for the Royal Family's amusements. The ceiling by Jean-Baptiste de Champaigne shows "Mercury in his Chariot;" "Alexander Greeting an Indian Embassy;" in the archings "Ptolemey Speaking to the Learned Men," "Augustus Greeting an Indian Embassy" and "Alexander Gathering Animals from All Parts of the World." Gobelins tapestries forming part of the History of the King tapestry and Savonnerie carpet. The famous clock with automatons was presented to Louis XIV by the clock-maker Morand, and the two fine chests of drawers were furnished by Boulle in 1709 for the King's bedchamber at Trianon. Over the door, "Apollo and Daphne" by Antoine Coypel and "Acis and Galatea" by Michel Corneille.

THE MARS DRAWING ROOM ▲ THE WAR DRAWING ROOM ▼

THE APOLLO DRAWING ROOM (9)

The ceiling, by Charles de La Fosse, shows "The Chariot of the Sun" surrounded by the Four Corners of the Earth, and the arch mouldings: "Coriolanus Raises the Siege of Rome,". "Vespasian Building the Colosseum," "Augustus Building the Port of Misenum" and "Porus Before Alexander." Over the door, "Allegory of the Dauphin's Birth" by Gabriel Blanchard and "Renown Bringing the King's Glory to the Four Corners of the Earth."

This room was used as the Throne Room. The silver throne, three metres high, was at the back, on a platform and under a dais: the site is now marked by a tapestry with threads of gold which is an allegory of Fire. The other two tapestries represent "The Audience Granted do Cardinal Chigi at Fontainebleau, on July 29, 1664" and "The Amends Made by Count de Fuentes on Behalf of the King of Spain, on March 2, 1662." Savonnerie carpet.

Over the mantelpiece, portrait of Louis XIV painted by Rigaud in 1701; opposite, that of Louis XV by Rigaud in 1730. The gilded wood candelabra were made in 1769 for the Hall of Mirrors (see below).

THE WAR DRAWING ROOM (10)

At first this room was the King's State Cabinet, the ceiling of which was later moved into the Queen's Guard Room (cf. p. 26); beyond it were two other cabinets opening onto a terrace set in the middle of the facade.

The terrace and the rooms around it disappeared in 1678 when the Hall of Mirrors was built; the War Drawing Room took its present form at that time: the walls are lined with marble and mirrors; on the mantelpiece there is a magnificent bas-relief by Antoine Coysevox showing Louis XIV triumphing over his enemies; on the vault Charles Le Brun pictured the Empire. Spain and Holland uniting against France.

THE HALL OF MIRRORS (11)

Seventy-nine yards long, more than eleven yards wide and over thirteen yards high, this wonderful room is without a doubt one of the marvels of the Château. The Vault paintings are by Le Brun who magnificently recalled the most glorious actions of the first eighteen years of the personal reign of Louis XIV. This work was carried out amidst the gilded stucco frames and decorations in "trompe-l'œil," military victories, administrative and economic reforms, etc.

The Pyrénées marble pilasters, the gilded bronze trophies, the seventeen mirror-lined arcades corresponding to the seventeen windows, create a majestic air.

The Hall is embellished with eight busts of Roman emperors in porphyry and marble, and eight statues, seven of which are antique: Bacchus, Venus, Chastity, Hermes, the Venus of Troas, Uranus and Nemesis. The eighth, a Diana sculptured by Frémin for the Marly gardens, occupies the place of the famous "Diana of Versailles," now in the Louvre.

THE HALL OF MIRRORS

The gilded candelabras are exact copies of the originals (now in the Apollo Drawing Room) which were ordered by Louis XV in 1769.

White gold-embroidered damask curtains and tables bearing precious vases completed the decoration of this Hall, which provided an incomparable setting for the Court's festivities and the audiences granted by the King to ambassadors extraordinary.

Different doors give access to the King's Suite (cf. p. 28): the first one leads to the Council Chamber, the others to the Second Antechamber.

THE QUEEN'S SUITE

THE PEACE DRAWING ROOM (12)

This drawing room was connected to the Queen's Suite and was used as the Gaming Room. Every Sunday, Marie Leczinska organised chamber music and choir concerts here.

The vault paintings by Le Brun show France granting peace to three defeated powers while above the mantle-piece François Le Moyne painted Louis XV in all his splendour at age seventeen, giving peace to Europe.

THE QUEEN'S BEDCHAMBER (13)

Three Queen's of France and two Dauphinesses have occupied this bedroom; nineteen princes and princesses of the House of France were born here.

The magnificent woodwork was executed for Marie Leczinska, as was the decoration of the ceiling, on which François Boucher painted the allegories of the Queen's Virtues, and the overdoors where De Troy and Natoire painted her children.

Marie Leczinska died in this room on June 24, 1768. Marie-Antoinette lived in it in her turn until October 6, 1789. The furnishings—"lampas" wall hangings, bed and chairs upholstered in embroidered silks—have been scrupulously restored as they were on the day when the last Queen of France left the Palace for the last time.

On the console-table, bust of Marie-Antoinette by Lecomte. The sumptuous mahogany jewel-case, adorned with mother-of-pearl and gilded bronze, was made by Schwerdfeger in 1787.

Two little doors in the alcove give access to the *QUEEN'S PRIVY CHAMBERS,* gathered around inner courtyards; two drawing-rooms (the exquisite Sofa Chamber (14) and the Gilded Chamber), two libraries, a dressing-room, a bathroom, a dining-room, a billiard and some service quarters. They allowed the Queen to have some semblance of private life beside her official duties. (Guided tour).

THE PRIVY CHAMBER OR GILDED CHAMBER (15)

This elegant drawing room where the Queen liked to invite her friends, was decorated, as we see it today, in 1783. The lovely woodwork, its neoclassical style softened by the late XVIIIth century gracefulness, was done by the Rousseau Brothers from designs by Richard Mique. For want of the original furniture, unfortunately scattered during the Revolution, we can at least see some handsome pieces from the old royal furniture a few pieces of which belonged to Marie-Antoinette herself.

THE QUEEN'S BEDCHAMBER ▲ THE PRIVY CHAMBER OR GILDED CHAMBER ▼

THE DRAWING ROOM OF THE NOBLES (16)

This was where the Queen held her circle and received ambassadors. Here also high-born women would be presented to her.

The ceiling by Michel Corneille shows "Mercury Escorted by Poetry and the Sciences;" in the archings some of the most culturel women of Antiquity are recalled: Sappho, Penelope, Aspasia, and Cesisena.

The fire-place, the wall-hangings and the handsome furniture made by Riesener and Gouthière were commissioned in 1785 by Marie-Antoinette. We can see a tapestry portrait of Louis XV by Van Loo, paintings by Boucher, above the doors are "Pygmalion" and "The Origin of Painting" by Regnault.

THE QUEEN'S ANTECHAMBER (17)

During the eighteenth century, the royal family supped here in state. The ceiling paintings represent Antique heroines celebrated for their martial virtue. The military musical instruments on the lintels are by Madeleine de Boulogne. Famous portrait of Marie-Antoinette and her children, by Madame Vigée Le Brun.

THE QUEEN'S GUARD ROOM (18)

All the paintings in this handsome room done by Noël Coypel are devoted of the legend of Jupiter excepting those on the archings which recall The Justice of Trajan, of Solon, of Alexander Severius, of Ptolemy Philidelphius.

The QUEEN'S STAIRCASE (19), by which one may leave, leads also, through a loggia, to the King's Suite (cf. p. 28). The loggia opens onto the former suite of Madame de Maintenon, where on can see mainly XVIth century (Guided tour).

THE CORONATION ROOM (20)

Former Grand Guard Room of the palace, this huge room was decorated as we see it today under Louis-Philippe in order to house three paintings showing important moments of Napoleonic history: "The Battle of Aboukir" by Gros; "The Coronation," and "The Distribution of Eagles," both by David. The ceiling is the work of Callet and the allegories on the lintels are by Gerard.

In the next room (21) the "Suppliers to the Crown" used to lay out their wares here. Louis-Philippe transformed it into the 1792 Drawing Room, collecting in one place the portraits of famous people during the Revolution and the Empire, painted as they were when the Monarchy fell.

THE PRINCES' STAIRCASE (22)

Dates back to Louis XIV; it led to the princes' suites on the second and first floors of the south wing.

THE BATTLE GALLERY (23)

This Gallery and the following "1830 ROOM" (actually closed for restoration) take up the whole second floor and the attic of the South Wing. One hundred and thirty yards long and over fourteen yards wide, it was created by Louis-Philippe in 1837 where four royal princes' suites used to be. The paintings recall the greatest victories of French history, from Tolbiac to Wagram.

THE ROOM OF THE NOBLES ▲

THE QUEEN'S STAIRCASE ▼

THE KING'S SUITE

(Guided tours by National Museums lecturers)

In 1684, Louis XIV moved into the rooms which, on the second floor of the Old Chateau, stand around the Marble Courtyard. At his death, the suite was occupied by Louis XV then Louis XVI, who both made noticeable changes in the decoration, especially in the privy chambers.

The loggia of the Queen's Staircase gives access to the GUARD ROOM (24), where the King's Bodyguards stayed. The FIRST ANTECHAMBER (25), where Louis XIV supped every evening with the Royal Family, in state, to the strains of the "Symphonies for the King's Supper", is decorated with paintings by Parrocel.

The SECOND ANTECHAMBER (26), also called the "Bull's-Eye Window Drawing Room", replaced in 1701 two rooms which had been an Antechamber and the King's Bedchamber. At that time, the large gilded frieze was carved to show children at play. The walls are hung with royal portraits and a large picture in which Jean Nocret painted Louis XIV and the royal family as the Olympian gods. The busts are Louis XIV by Coysevox, Louis XV by Gois and Louis XVI by Houdon.

In this antechamber, the courtiers waited to be allowed into the King's Bedchamber for the "Lever" and retiring ceremonies.

THE KING'S BEDCHAMBER (27)

Placed in the centre of the royal suite, on a line with the Avenue de Paris, this beautiful room was at first a drawing room opening onto the Hall of Mirrors through three arcades. In 1701, Louis XIV chose to make it his bedchamber and, at that time, Nicholas Coustou carved the bas-relief in the alcove picturing "France Watching over the Sleeping King;" the furniture was covered in crimson velvet with gold embroidery in winter and with crimson gold and silver brocade in summer. Above the doors are portraits of the Marquis de Moncade and Van Dyck by Van Dyck, a "St. John the Baptist" by Carraciolo and a "Mary-Magdalene" by Dominiquin; in the attic: "The Four Evangelists" and "The Tribute Money" by Valentin and "Hagar in the Desert" by Lanfranco. On the mantle-piece is a handsome bust of Louis XIV by Coysevox.

Louis XIV died in this room on September 1st, 1715 and his successors used it as a state room. On the morning of October 6, 1789, Louis XVI and Marie-Antoinette appeared on the balcony at the demand of the Parisians gathered in the Marble Court; a few hours later they left Versailles, never to return.

THE KING'S CHAMBER OR COUNCIL CHAMBER (28)

This room was the centre of political life in old France: here the King would preside over the Cabinet meetings every day, here he would grant his private audiences, here he would receive the oaths of allegiance from the High Crown Officers and here he would hold the Order of the Holy Spirit Councils.

THE KING'S BEDCHAMBER ▲

THE COUNCIL CHAMBER ▼

The magnificent wood panels were carved in 1755 by Antoine Rousseau from designs by Gabriel. On the mantlepiece, is an extraordinary clock made in 1754 for Louis XV and two vases that Louis XVI commissioned Thomire to do for this mantlepiece.

The porphyry bust of Alexander the Great and the bronze bust of Scipio Africanus were placed in this room by Louis XV.

One of the doors opens onto the suite of the *KING'S PRIVY CHAMBERS.* At the time of Louis XIV, they kept the most precious items of the royal collections: vases adorned with precious stones, gold coins and famous paintings such as "Mona Lisa" by Leonardo da Vinci.

Transformed by Louis XV, in 1738, into a private apartment, these rooms allowed the King to work, alone or with his councellers, and to receive his personal friends away from the uproar of the State Apartment. A new decoration, including carved and gilded wood panels, by Verberckt, was then created from designs by Gabriel.

Louis XIV's former billiard-room was turned into a *BEDCHAMBER (29)* in 1738 by Louis XV who thereafter used Louis XIV's Bedchamber (27) only for the daily "Lever" and Retiring ceremonies; he died here on May 10, 1774, and Louis XVI lived here until October 6, 1789.

On the mantlepiece is a bust of the Duchess ot Burgundy, Louis XV's mother, by Coysevox.

A little door in the alcove gives access to a small study, the wonderful panels of which have been carved for Louis XVI by the Rousseau brothers.

The *DOG CHAMBER (30)* was used as an antechamber for the inner suite valets, called "blue boys" because of their livery. The woodwork dates back to 1684 and comes from Louis XIV's former private billiard room.

This antechamber opens onto the *KING'S STAIRCASE (31),* whose the wrought iron railing is adorned with Louis XV's monogram and which allowed the King to leave his private apartment without going through the State Apartment. This elegant staircase leads, on the ground floor, to a small *GUARD ROOM* outside which, on January 5, 1757, Damiens attacked Louis XV.

The *HUNTERS' DINING ROOM (32)* looking to the Stag Court, was furnished in 1750. Louis XV would sup here twice a week with some of the lords and ladies from the hunt. We should notice the Sèvres porcelain plaques commissioned by Louis XVI copying "Louis XV Hunting" by d'Oudry.

The *CLOCK CHAMBER (33)* owes its name to the famous astronomical clock placed here in 1754 by Louis XV and still admired today. This clockwork masterpiece was designed by the engineer Passemant and built by Dauthiau; the bronzework was chased by Jacques Caffieri. In the middle of the room is a statue of Louis XV on horseback by Vassé, a scale model of the Bouchardon statue which stood in the center of the Louis XV Square in Paris before the Revolution. There are magnificent carved and gilded tables with stucco trays representing the maps of the main Crown lands. Barometer which belonged to Louis XVI.

The Clock Chamber was used as a Gaming Room in the evening and as an antechamber to the King's study during the day.

THE CLOCK CHAMBER ▲

THE KING'S STUDY ▼

THE KING'S STUDY (34)

This was Louis XV's favourite room where he would usually work and grant private audiences. It is also the most beautiful room of the inner suite and happily, has come down to us almost intact with its marvelous woodwork and its extraordinary furnishings: a roll-top writing desk by Oeben and Riesener; a chest-medal cabinet by Gaudreaux, corner cupboards by Joubert. The eighteenth century in France undoubtedly never produced anything richer or more elegant.

It was to the *BACK CHAMBER (35)* next door that Louis XV retired to write his instructions to his agents abroad or to study their reports. This then was the seat of the "King's Secret," his private diplomatic policy led without the knowledge of anyone else.

Under Louis XIV there was a Small Gallery further on, flanked by two drawing rooms. The vaults of these three rooms were painted by Mignard and the King kept his most prized paintings there. The whole suite was torn down by Louis XV in 1752 at the same time as the Ambassadors' Stairway just behind the Small Gallery and replaced by a suite for the King's eldest daughter, Princess Marie-Adelaïde who lived here until 1769. The King then took it back for his own use and only the *PRIVY CHAMBER (36)* of the Princess remains. Its woodwork recalls her taste for music and here, in December 1763, the child Mozart played for the royal family.

Just beside it Louis XV had a *BATHROOM* installed with lovely woodwork recalling the pleasures of waterplay.

THE LOUIS XVI LIBRARY (37)

Louis XIV decided to install this tasteful room as soon as he came to the throne. The King liked to work here at a small desk set in a window recess.

The quietly elegant woodwork was done by Antoine Rousseau, from drawings of Gabriel; the handsome round table was made by Riesener especially for this room the seats covered in "pékin" were used by Louis XVI himself.

THE CHINA DRAWING ROOM (38) was used as a dining-room during the last years of the Monarchy. At Christmas, the most beautiful pieces of china produced at the Sèvres Manufacture that year were displayed.

The next room, defaced by Louis-Philippe when he built the neighbouring stairway over an inner courtyard, used to be the *BILLIARD ROOM.*

THE LOUIS XVI GAMING ROOM (39)

This is the former "Rare Objects Cabinet" under Louis XIV (cf. above, p. 18) transformed first into an Antechamber for Madame Adelaïde then into a Game Room.

Most of the handsome furniture has been brought back and put into place: Riesener corner cupboards, carved and gilded chairs. The crimson and gold brocade was rewoven in Lyons. The Van Blarenberghe gouache paintings picturing Louis XV's campaigns have been hung back on their former places on the walls.

THE LOUIS XVI LIBRARY ▲

THE LOUIS XVI GAMING ROOM ▼

MADAME DU BARRY'S SUITE

(Guided tour by National Museums lecturers)

In 1728, Louis XV had a Small Suite installed above his Privy Chamber and all around the Stag Court. It comprised several drawing rooms, dining-rooms, libraries, laboratories, workshops, kitchens, aviaries and terraces. He glady stole away here, alone or with a few friends, escaping the rigid court etiquette to live as any private individual.

In 1766, at the death of the Dauphin, he gave the suite to the Dauphiness, Marie-Josephe de Saxe, who died here on March 13, 1767. Two years later, he gave it to Madame Du Barry who lived here until the King's death in 1774.

THE MADAME DU BARRY DRAWING ROOM

Placed above the Clock Chamber, it is embellished by charming woodwork as are the other rooms of this suite. Madame Du Barry had collected rich and elegant furnishings here, all sold during the Revolution. The beautiful seats we can see today come from the former royal collections and may have belonged to her.

The drawing room is in the middle of the suite which also includes a bedchamber, a game-room, a dining-room, a library, two antechambers, a bath-room and wardrobes.

THE ROYAL OPERA (40)

(Guided tour by National Museums lecturers)

Until this magnificient opera house was built, the French Court had to make do with temporary theatres. It was only in 1768 that Louis XV commissioned the present one, inaugurated by the Wedding festivities for the Dauphin, the future Louis XVI and the Archduchesse Marie-Antoinette on May 16, 1770.

Ange-Jacques Gabriel, the architect, built one of his masterpices here: the ingenious truncated oval design, the harmonious proportions, the beautiful Pajou sculptures, the delicately tinted false marble, the velvets and silks make this Opera the most beautiful theatre in all the world.

Defaced during the nineteenth century by a coat of red paint, transformed in 1871 into a meeting room for the National Assembly, it has regained its former splendour today thanks to painstaking restoration.

COUNTESS DU BARRY'S ROOM ▲ THE ROYAL OPERA ▼

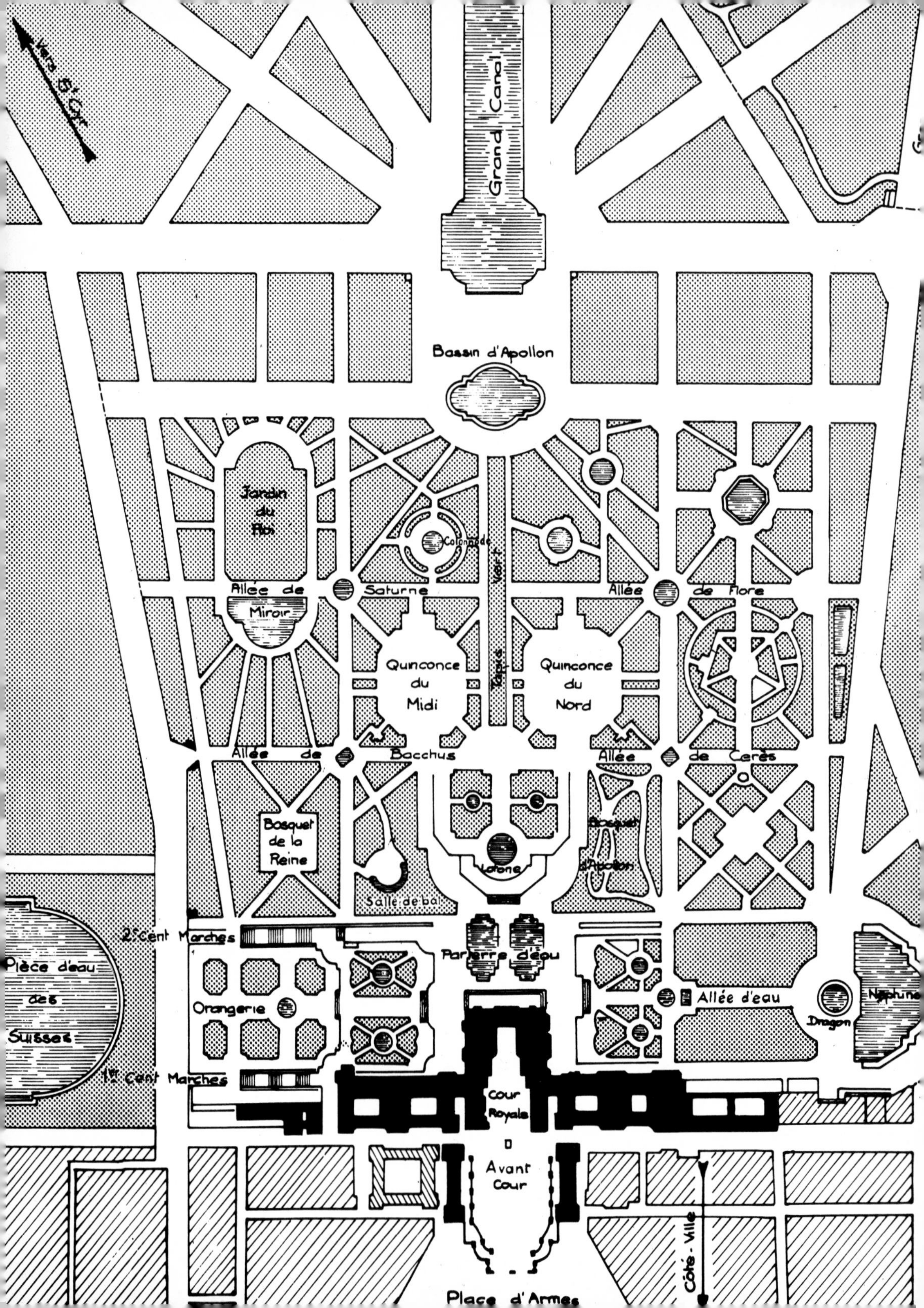

Vers St Cyr
Grand Canal
Bassin d'Apollon
Jardin du Roi
Colonnade
Allée de Miroir
Saturne
Allée de Flore
Quinconce du Midi
Quinconce du Nord
Tapis Vert
Allée de Bacchus
Allée de Cerès
Bosquet de la Reine
Salle de bal
Latone
Bosquet d'Apollon
2e Cent Marches
Parterre d'eau
Pièce d'eau des Suisses
Orangerie
Allée d'eau
Neptune
Dragon
1re Cent Marches
Cour Royale
Avant Cour
Côté Ville
Place d'Armes

OVERALL VIEW OF VERSAILLES ▲

THE MARBLE COURT ▼

THE GARDENS

OVERALL VIEW OF VERSAILLES

This aerial view enables us to see the brilliant design of Le Nôtre who managed to group around a large axial perspective the outlay of the town, the château and the gardens. In the foreground, are situated, the Latona, North and South parterres (flower beds) which frame the Water Basin. Further back is the Western facade and beyond that the courtyards, the parade ground and the three forked avenues, separated by the Grand and Small Stables.

THE MARBLE COURT (cf. p. 37)

This is the original Louis XIII lodge maintained but considerably embellished by Louis XIV. The King's Suite takes up the whole second floor: the three middle windows are the Bedchamber where Louis XIV died, the right wing is taken up by the King's Privy Chambers; above is Madame Du Barry's Suite. The lead of the roofs were all originally gilded.

THE MAIN BUILDING SEEN FROM THE WATER BASIN

This noble front, rhythmed by columned fore-parts and crowned by a balustrade, trophies and fire ornaments bears eloquent witness to the Italian influence on seventeenth-century French architecture.

The buildings, erected by Louis Le Vau, from 1668 onwards, surround the former lodge of Louis XIII on three sides. In the centre of the facade at that time a terrace separated the King's Suite on the left and the Queen's Suite on the right: we can still see traces of it on the present facade completed in 1678 by Jules Hardouin-Mansard.

On the main floor, the Hall of Mirrors extends between the War Drawing Room to the left and the Peace Drawing Room to the right. On the ground floor to either side of the Low Gallery, on the left the former Bathing Suite of Louis XIV that Louis XV made into a suite for his daughter, Madame Victoire; on the right the Dauphin's Suite.

The statues erected on the fore-parts represent Apollo and Diana surrounded by the Twelve Months of the Year; in the recesses are Art and Nature joining to beautify the Sun King's Gardens. The masks decorating the ground floor arcades recall the different ages of man; from childhood on the right to old age on the left. The four bronzes statues were cast from four famous antique models: Bacchus, the Apollo of the Belvedere, Mercury and Silenus. On the corners of the perron are the vase of War by Coysevox and the vase of Peace by Tuby.

The Water Basin attained its present aspect between 1684 and 1690. The bronze statues decorating the marble curbstones of the two large basins make an exceptionnally beautiful group. Represented in the four corners are the four largest French rivers, each of which is accompanied by its main tributary: to the North, near the castle, are the Garonne and the Dordogne by Coysevox;

THE MAIN BUILDING SEEN FROM THE WATER BASIN ▲

THE SOUTH FLOWER BED ▼

to the South the Loire and the Loiret by Regnaudin; near the Latona stairs to the North are the Seine (shown in the photo) and the Marne by Le Hongre; to the South the Rhône and the Saône by Tuby. Groups of children and water-nymphs complete the arrangement.

THE MAIN BUILDING SEEN FROM THE SOUTH PARTERRES

On the main floor to the right of the Peace Drawing Room in the angle is the Queen's Suite; on the ground floor are the State Chamber and the Dauphin's Library which can be recognized by its brightly coloured shutters, then the Dauphiness's Suite.

The statues in the recesses represent Music and Dance; those of the fore-parts represent Flora, Zephir, Vertumma, Pomona, Thalia, Terpsiechore, etc.

Lovely bronze vases line the South flower bed which has kept its original primitive design. We reach it by crossing a perron hight of steeps flanked by two Cupids riding sphinxes.

THE ORANGERIE GROVE AND THE SWISS GUARD LAKE

The South Grove ends on a terrace looking out over the Orangery. Beyond its rows of orange trees, pomegranates and palm trees we catch a glimpse of the Swiss Guard Lake, the largest ornamental lake after the Grand Canal: measuring 739 1/2 yards by 253 yards, it was dug between 1678 and 1681 by the Swiss Guard Regiment, hence its name. At its southern end, at the foot of the Satory Woods, stands the equestrian statue of Louis XIV by Lorenzo Bernini.

In the middle of the row of trees along the left side of the lake, a wrought-iron gate opens onto the King's Kitchen-Garden which used to supply the Court with all sorts of fruits, vegetables and fresh products. It is still almost exactly like it was when La Quintinie designed and planted it.

THE ORANGERY GREENHOUSE

This gigantic building, as majestic as any of the great monuments of Antiquity was built by Jules Hardouin-Mansart between 1684 and 1686. It is made up of three vaulted galleries 42 feet high and 42 feet wide, the longest measuring over 168 yards. During the winter they house over a thousand orange trees palm trees and pomegranates that decorate the Orangery flower bed in the summertime. Sunken on the North side and wide open to the South, the Greenhouse is never heated and yet the temperature never drops below 43° F. Large scale levelling was needed to build the platform of the Southern parterre which is kept in place by the Orangery Greenhouse and can be reached by descending the two monumental hundred steps staircases.

The Greenhouse makes a powerful foundation for the château's long facade. The South or Princes' Wing we see from here included the Children of France Suite and the Governess Suite on the ground floor. The main floor was for the four suites intended for the royal Princes under Louis XIV, it housed his brother and sister-in-law, the Duke and Duchess of Orleans, as well as the Duke of Chartres, the future Regent and his wife; under Louis XVI the Count and Countess of Artois, the King's brother and sister-in-law, and his sister, Madame Elizabeth, lived here.

THE ORANGERIE GROVE ▲

THE ORANGERY GREENHOUSE ▼

Coming back towards the Water Parterre, we climb the "Three steps of pink marble" as described by the poet Alfred de Musset and walk along the balustrade at the end of which stands the statue of Ariadne, copied from the famous Vatican antique, after which we come to the Fountain of Daybreak. The marble basin is adorned with two bronze groups representing animal combats and flanked by a statue of "Water" by Le Gros and "Spring" by Magnier.

Unlike the South Parterre, which is horizontal, the North Parterre slopes gently. This slope permitted the construction of a descending series of basins throught which the water flows downwards until it reaches the Basin of Neptune. While the South Parterre is widely exposed to the sun, the North Parterre is closed off by high leafage that shelters the flowers from the cold. Two sides are lined with some of the twenty-four statues sculpted from 1674 on by some of the period's most famous artists, based on designs by Le Brun. These statues, originally intented for the Water Basin represent "the Four Seasons," "the Four Times of Day," "the Four Elements," "the Four Continents," "the Four Poems," and "the Four Humours"—in short, everything in the Universe that is influenced by the course of the sun.

LANE OF THREE FOUNTAINS

This name comes from the Grove, no longer existing, that used to be along this lane. It begins from the Diana Chamber or Eventide Fountain decorated with animal combats and slopes down along the North Parterre. After Le Hongre's beautiful "Ether" (not shown in the photo) we come across "Diana" or "Eventide" by Desjardins, then "Venus" or "Noontide" by Gaspard Marsy, "Europe" by Mazeline, "Africa" by Sybraique, "Night" by Raon, "Earth" by Massou, and the "Pastoral" by Granier. Other statues commissioned at the same time line the far end of the flower bed: "Autumn" by Regnaudin, "America" by Guerin, "Summer" by Hutinot, "Winter" by Girardon, one of the loveliest in this group, and finally the "Heroic Poem" which was sculpted by Drouilly in the likeness of Louis XIV.

At the end of the North Flower Bed, the two Crown Basins precede the elegant Pyramid Fountain with ornaments by Girardon: tritons, dolphins and crayfish. This fountain overlooks Diana bathing with the Nymphs bas-relief also by Girardon who created here a masterpiece of sensual grace.

THE TWILIGHT WATER LANE

This lane is one of Le Nôtre's most charming creations in Versailles, it slopes down from the North Parterre towards the Dragon Basin and is lined with marble bowl fountain each upheld by a bronze arrangement showing three laughing children. At the top of the lane can be seen the silhouette of the Pyramid Fountain and the main building of the château. In the woods to the left once stood the Arch of Triumph Grove, but today the "Triumphal France" arrangement remains.

The far end of this lane curves out into a spreading promenade bordered by more child-borne fountains. The Dragon Basin in the centre has the most powerful waterworks system in the whole gardens.

The Neptune Basin which closes the Water Lane perspective was only decorated under Louis XV; it includes mainly three arrangements in lead: in

THE LANE OF TREE FOUNTAINS ▲

THE TWILIGHT WATER LANE ▼

the centre "Neptune and Amphitrite" by L. S. Adam; to the left "Proteus" by Bouchardon; to the right "the Ocean" by J. B. Lemoine. The 99 fountains of the Neptune Basin offer a truly breathtaking spectacle reserved for the grand final of the waterworks display.

THE LATONA BASIN AND FLOWER BED

The general theme in the decor of the Versailles gardens is taken from the legend of Apollo. This basin recalls the events of the birth of this god and of his twin sister, Diana: their mother, Latona, insulted by Lycian peasants, begs for justice from her lover, Jupiter, who turns them into lizards and frogs.

Beyond the flower bed extend the *ROYAL DRIVE* and the Grand Canal. On either side, two stairs lead down to the lower level; they are lined with statues, mostly copies of antiques commissioned in Rome by Louis XIV. Together with the statues in the flower beds and the groves, they make the Versailles gardens an extraordinary museum of seventeenth century French sculpture.

On either side of the main line formed by the *ROYAL DRIVE,* the tall woods are plotted out by six lanes: two run parallel to the axis, four run perpendicularly; their intersections are marked by four basins, the Four Seasons, and they form the boundaries of thickly wooded squares where the Groves are hidden.

THE BALLROOM GROVE

This grove is embellished with rockword and shells partly masked by seventeen cascades when the fountains are playing. Eight gilded lead vases and candelabra give it the look of an open-air salon. Louis XIV sometimes gave balls in this grove, and the guests danced on a central marble platform which no longer exists.

The *QUEEN'S GROVE* replaced, under Louis XVI, the Maze, the winding paths of which were marked by thirty-nine tinted lead fountains depicting Aesop's Fables.

After the Bacchus or Autumn Basin by the Marsy brothers, we come to the Farthingale then the King's Garden which replaced the royal Isle Basin under Louis XVIII.

The Saturn or Winter Basin by Girardon is near the *CHESTNUT TREE ARBOUR* which in 1704, replaced the Antiques Arbour where the King used to display some of the antiques from his collection admist the fountains and the orange trees.

THE COLONNADE GROVE

This circular peristyle, 104 feet in diameter, was the work of Jules Hardouin-Mansart. The twenty-four Pyrénées marble columns (state blue, Languedoc, violet brecchia) carry white marble arcades under which the fountains of twenty-eight basins play. The finest sculptors decorated the arcade cornerstones with children's games.

In the centre Louis XIV had placed the famous "Rape of Proserpine" sculpture, Girardon's masterpiece. It was recently removed to protect it against the weather.

THE LATONA BASIN ▲

THE BALLROOM GROVE ▼

THE ROYAL DRIVE (COVER)

This majestic avenue is sometimes called the Green Carpet. It extends from the Latona flower bed to the Apollo Basin and is lined with vases and statues. The vases, among the most original products of the Versailles school are alternately decorated with lilies, sunflowers, cornucopia, oak and laurel branches. The statues are primarily copies of antique works such as the Medici Venus by Frémery seen here.

The Royal Drive leads to a hemicycle bordered by terms and two marble arrangements: on the left "Ino and Melicertes" by Garnier; on the right "Aristaeus and Proteus" by Slodtz.

Beyond the Apollo Basin, the Grand Canal closes the main perspective. The long arm of this cross-shaped canal measures over 1,787 yards long and 67 yards wide; the short arm, which extends on the right toward the Trianon, is 1,159 yards long and over 87 yards wide. The Canal's perimeter is 4.2 miles.

THE APOLLO BASIN

The Grand Waterworks display is an unequalled sight. The gushing forth of all the fountains completes the silhouette of the basins and fountains, animates them with a quivering that joins the delights of light to the joys of water. In the Old Regime, the lakes and fountains visible from the château windows played all day long, but the grove fountains were turned on only when the King would go by them.

At opposite ends of the Royal Drive, the Latona and Apollo Basins take on their full meaning: especially in the second one, the Sun Chariot of Tuby seems to spring out of the waves before beginning its glorious course across the skies.

From the Apollo Basin we can go directly to Trianon. However, particularly on the days of the Waterworks Show it is better to walk back up towards the château through the North Groves.

The *ENCELADUS GROVE* recalls the legend of the giant who wanted to climb Mount Olympus. The *DOMA GROVE* owes its name to two marble and gilded bronze pavilions no longer standing; two marble balustrades surround the basin as well eight statues including Tuby's noteworthy "Acis and Galatea."

The Flora or Spring Basin by Tuby leads to the *OBELISK.* From here through the *STAR GROVE,* we come to the lovely Isle of Bliss Basin behind which a Green Circle marks the site of the *WATER THEATRE* which used to display the most unheard of hydraulic tricks.

Past the Ceres or Summer Basin by Regnaudin we come to the *APOLLO BATHING GROVE* decorated as we see it today under Louis XVI; Hubert Robert designed the romantic grotto sheltering the works which Louis XIV commissioned from Girardon, Regnaudin, by Marsy and Guérin; "Nymphs of Thetis Waiting on Apollo" and "The Tritons Grooming the Sun Chariot Horses."

We exit through the far end of the North Parterre and on to the Water Lane and Neptune Basin (cf. above p. 42).

THE COLONNADE ▲

THE APOLLO BASIN ▼

TRIANON

The name comes from a Hamlet dating back to the Middle Ages which Louis XIV purchased in order to enlarge his estate. In 1670 he built here a pavilion covered with blue and white china, called "the China Trianon," which he enclosed with delightful gardens. In 1687 this all too fragile pavilion was demolished to make room for the present little marble palace designed by Mansart.

THE PALACE OF TRIANON

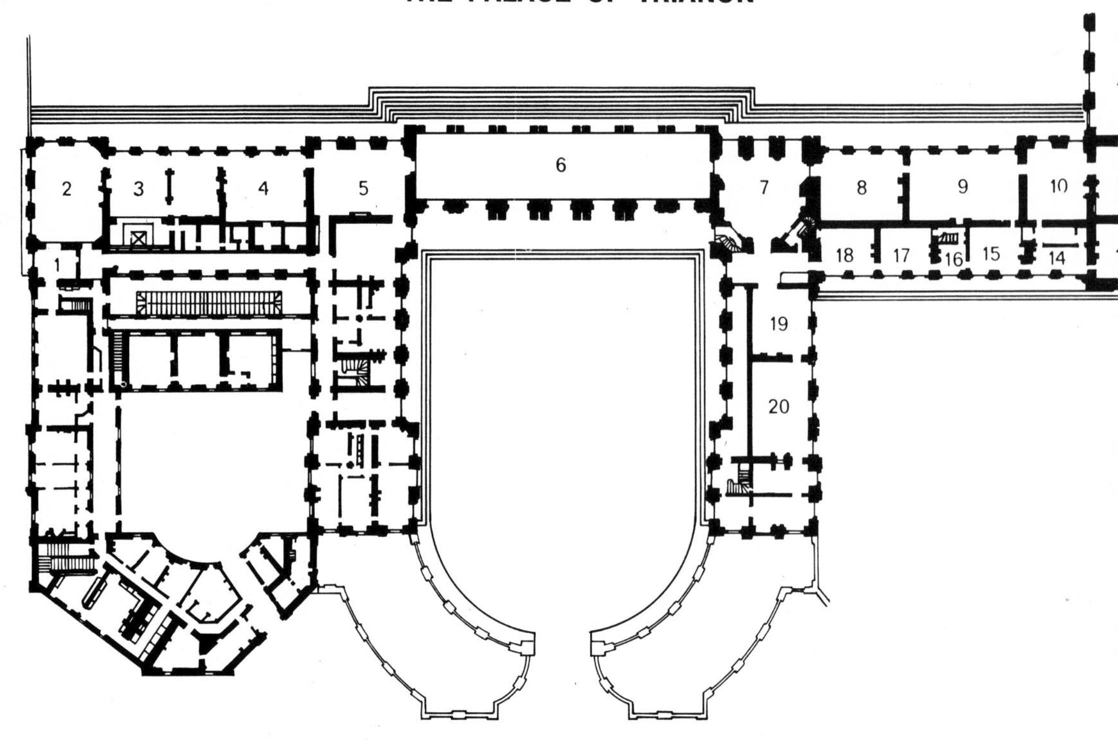

1 - Boudoir
2 - The Mirror Chamber
3 - The Bedroom
4 - The Antechamber of the Chapel
5 - The Hall of Nobles
6 - The Peristyle
7 - The circular Salon
8 - The Music Salon
9 - The Family Salon
10 - The Malachite Salon
11 - The cool Salon
12 - The Gallery
13 - The Springs Salon
14 - The Antechamber
15 - The Study
16 - The Bath Apartment
17 - The Bedroom
18 - "Salon du déjeûn" (The Breakfast Room)
19 - The Salon
20 - The Bedroom

THE ROYAL COURTYARD ▲

THE FACADE ON THE GARDENS ▼

A sunk-fence and a low gate separate the fore-court from the main court; the side wings are connected by a "Peristyle" through which one can see the gardens. The very elegant architecture of this modest single-story structure is brightened by the marble pilasters and columns and enhanced by delicately carved ornaments.

The centre of the Garden Facade is marked by the peristyle colonnade. To the right extends the King's Suite which was later to become the Dauphin's, then, during the Napoleonic era, Marie-Louise's. Over to our left begin the Reception Rooms, which were later to become Napoleon's State Suite. The wing at right angles contains the Gallery, prolonged by the Garden Drawing Room from where the wing of Trianon-in-the-Woods extends. The flowers in the beds blend in perfect harmony with the colour of the marble; during the reign of Louis XIV new flowers were planted daily.

The Trianon was out of bounds to courtiers, being the King's Private Hide-Away, a hide-away where he would enjoy peace and quiet with his family. Stripped bare during the Revolution, Napoleon had it restored and refurnished. He came to stay a number of times with his spouse, the Empress Marie-Louise (1).

THE LEFT WING

This wing contains a suite which was occupied by Louis XIV, the Dauphin, his son, Marie Leczinska and, during the nineteenth century, Madame Mère (the mother of Napoleon I), the Empress Marie-Louise, Queen Marie-Amélie. The usual entrance to the left wing was through the peristyle. Today the tour is conducted in the opposite direction. After having crossed a drawing room the visitor proceeds down a hall leading to Marie-Louise's Boudoir.

THE MIRROR CHAMBER (2)

This beautiful room, with its marvelous view overlooking the grand canal, was used for several years as a Council Chamber for Louis XIV. Its carved woodwork and mirrors date back to that time.

During the Napoleonic era, the Empress used it as a study. Her pianoforte, drawing table and work table can still be seen here.

THE KING'S BEDCHAMBER (3)

For some time Louis XIV's bedchamber, it was later occupied by his son, the Dauphin. In 1770 it was adorned with columns and woodwork which make it one of the most beautiful rooms of the palace. Under Napoleon it was divided into a small-sized bedchamber and drawing room for Madame Mère then for the Empress Marie-Louise and for Queen Marie-Amélie. It has now been restored to its original size.

The furniture belonged to Marie-Louise with the exception of the bed which was made for Napoleon at the Tuileries and brought over for Queen Marie-Amélie. The paintings of flowers are by Monnoyer and Blain de Fontenay.

THE MIRROR CHAMBER ▲

THE KING'S BEDCHAMBER ▼

THE ANTECHAMBER OF THE CHAPEL (4) is embellished with a cornice with alternating wheatsheaves and bunches of grapes, paintings of two of the Evangelists: here Louis XIV used to hear mass which was celebrated beyond the door at the far end of the room. Later it was to become the first Drawing Room to the Empress. The large inlaid pedestal table was brought in for her.

The first antechamber, formely *CHAMBER OF THE NOBLES (5)* is furnished with a teakwood table almost nine feet in diameter. Portraits of the Dauphin and his family, of Louis XV and Marie Leczinska.

Louis XIV himself conceived the *PERISTYLE (6)* which connects both wings and is in fact a kind of "Loggia" where the King would occasionally sup.

THE RIGHT WING

Bigger than its left counterpart, it contains the reception rooms as well as various suites where the King and most of his family lived. Napoleon had his state and privy suites here.

THE ROUND DRAWING ROOM (7) has a handsome décor of Corinthian columns and two paintings by Verdier. The door at the far end originally opened onto a theatre that Louis XIV did away with in 1703 and replaced by his new suite (cf. below, p. 56). During the reign of Napoleon the Round Drawing Room was called the Ushers' Room and became the first room of the Emperor's State Suite.

THE MUSIC ROOM (8) was originally the antechamber where Louis XIV would have his meals: the doors at the far end were crowned by a gallery where the musicians once stood. Napoleon turned it into the Officers' Drawing Room.

THE FAMILY DRAWING ROOM (9) occupies the area that was once two rooms: the Game Room and Bed room, later o become the Superior Officers' Drawing Room and the Princes' Drawing Room under Napoleon.

Louis-Philippe pulled down the wall between the two in order to make this large drawing room where the Royal Family used to gather in the evening. The Queen and Princesses would sit around the family tables and each one used to keep her needlework in one of the numbered drawers to which she had a key.

THE MALACHITE DRAWING ROOM (10)

The painting by La Fosse over the mantlepiece "Apollo with Thetis" is a reminder to us that this room was the Sunset chamber before becoming the bedchamber to the Duchess of Burgundy, mother of Louis XV.

Napoleon made it his State Chamber and adorned it with the sumptuous furnishing which we know today: seats and drapes of brocade-bordered crimson damask, ebony furniture by Jacob-Desmalter and, above all, the malachites offered by the Tzar Alexander I and mounted in bronze by Thomire.

THE MALACHITE DRAWING ROOM ▲

THE GALLERY ▼

THE COOL DRAWING ROOM (11) owes its name to its northern exposure; it was the Council Chamber of Napoleon and Charles X. The handsome woodwork and the views of Versailles painted by J. B. Martin prefigure the Gallery decoration.

THE GALLERY (12) which sheltered the flower beds against Northerly winds was primarily decorated by a series of twenty-four paintings, each depicting Versailles and the Trianon Gardens as they were in the days of Louis XIV: many a grove having disappeared, these works are priceless documents. The marble coolers originate from the Buffet Room of Louis XV (cf. below, p. 56); the beautiful chandeliers and furniture were placed during the reign of Napoleon.

THE GARDEN DRAWING ROOM (13) with its six windows opening onto alternating rows of trees and the Grand Canal perspective. Under Louis XIV there was a cross beam, under Napoleon a billiard table. Today it has been furnished as a drawing room for state receptions. It also leads to the Trianon-in-the-Woods wing which, under Louis XIV, housed the King's daughters, his brother and sister-in-law, the Palatine Princesse.

THE DRAWING ROOM OF THE SPRINGS (14) takes its name from the grove it overlooked and which disappeared under Louis XVI. It was used as an Antechamber by Madame de Maintenon, as a Map-Room by Napoleon.

THE EMPEROR'S PRIVY SUITE (15)

The adjoining rooms form the Emperor's Small Apartment which Napoleon obtained by combining the former apartment of Madame de Maintenon and a part of Louis XV's. The Antechamber occupies part of ther former Marquise's State Chamber.

THE EMPEROR'S STUDY (16)

This room was formely Madame de Maintenon's bedroom. It is the only room in the whole of Trianon where the decorations on the walls date back to Napoleon. It was furnished by order of the Emperor while he was faring war in Russia: the fire place was put in as well as the green brocade bordered damask on the walls. The paintings, on the other hand, are those which once hung in the suite of Madame de Maintenon.

Napoleon's Bathroom is the former Privy Chamber of Louis XV whose suite began here.

THE EMPEROR'S BEDCHAMBER (17)

Once the room of Louis XV—the fire place and woodwork dating back to that time—it was speedily refurnished for Napoleon who, following his divorce with Joséphine, went to think things over at Trianon. He then had hung on the walls the beautiful buff coloured watered silk with lilac and silver brocade borders. This exquisite work had been woven for the Empress's suite at the Tuileries.

Through the *SALON DU DEJEUN (18)* we come to the Suite that King Louis-Philippe had furnished for his daughter, the Queen of Belgium. Louis XIV dwelled here, his successor Louis XV established on the spot the principal rooms of his own suite.

Originally the small *ANTECHAMBER* and the *DRAWING ROOM (19)* made up one single room: Antechamber under Louis XIV, a Game-Room under Louis XV; under Napoleon a Drawing Room (19). The beautiful violet breccia fire-place was installed in 1750.

NAPOLEON'S STUDY ▲

THE EMPEROR'S BEDCHAMBER ▼

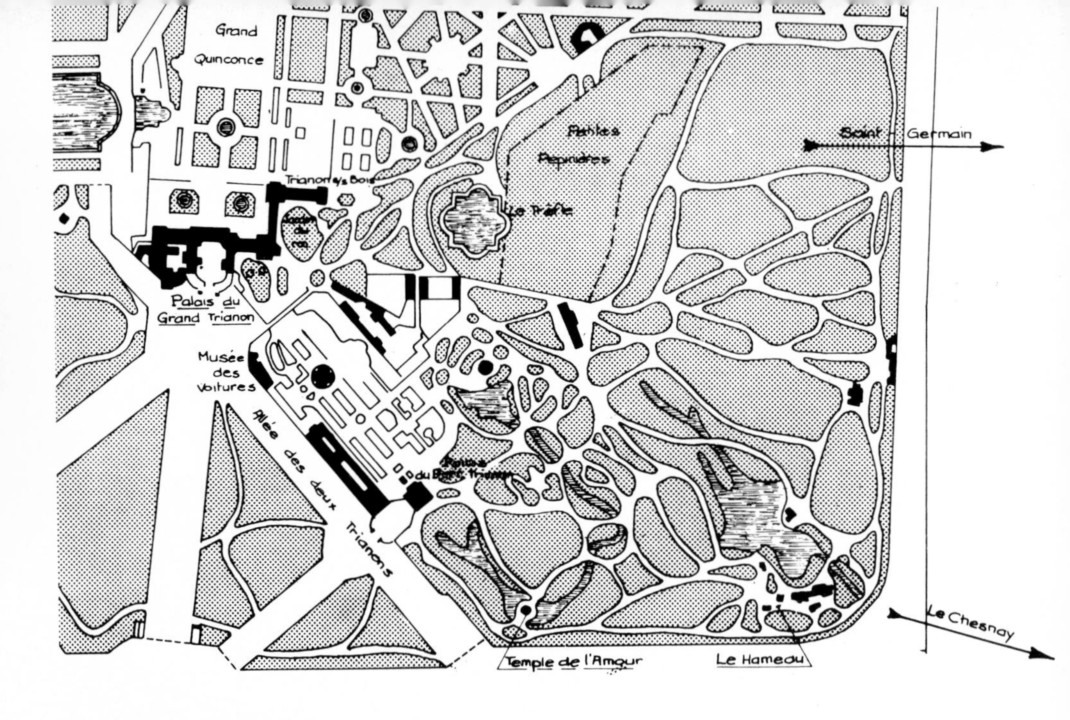

THE BEDCHAMBER (20) (once Louis XV's and later Napoleon's dining-room), was formed by joining together the Bedchamber and Privy Chamber of Louis XIV.

Originally the last two rooms were only one: first of all under Louis XIV a Council Chamber, then a Buffet Room during the next reign, hence the coolers in the gallery.

In the course of the first part of his reign, Louis XV did not seem very enraptured about Trianon: he went as far as giving it to the Queen who used it from time to time to lodge her father, ex-King Stanislas of Poland. From 1750 onwards he came more and more frequently and had it completely redecorated.

In a short span of time he undertook the transformation of part of the Park, building new constructions and drawing up the plans of a Botanical Garden. In order to destinguish this more recent building from what Louis XIV had created this creation bears the name of Petit Trianon (or Small Trianon).

THE SMALL TRIANON

Louis XV was fascinated by botany. In the garden at Trianon which he entrusted to Claude Richard he followed with a keen eye the experiments which were carried out there, especially the attempts of acclimatizing fig trees, coffee shrub and pineapples, as well as the cultivation of geraniums, china asters and strawberries. At his request the causes of wheat spoilage and the ways to combat it were studied. He also asked Jussieu to create a garden devoted to the study of plants (Jardin des Plantes), where for the first time the latter's new principles for classifying plants were applied. Finally the King bade his commodores bring him exotic plants for which hot houses were built. Between the botanical garden and the Palace of Trianon there is a garden in French style. It can be reached by a small bridge after a visit to the King's Private Garden where the tour of the Trianon should begin.

THE PAVILLON OF THE FRENCH GARDEN ▲ THE SMALL TRIANON CHATEAU ▼

THE PAVILION OF THE FRENCH GARDEN

This edifice was built by Gabriel in 1750 and stands in the middle of the French Garden, a charming example of French "rocaille" architecture. The mascarons of the arched windows depict the four seasons and the balustrade is enlivened by groups of children and vases with flowers. The interior comprises a circular salon with four rooms opening onto it: a Boudoir, Wardrobe, Kitchen, etc. The woodwork of the salon are the work of Verberckt and depict children's games: hunting, fishing, gardening; the farm yard animals on the cornice remind us of the neighbouring Menagerie.

The *MENAGERIE* Buildings, which can be seen towards the left, comprised a cowhouse, sheepfold, chicken pen and an aviary which housed livestock (cows, goats, ducks, chickens, etc.) bred for selective purposes.

To the right of the French Pavilion, where the King enjoyed taking refreshments, there once stood the *COOL SALON,* of which nothing today remains. It was a summertime dining-room.

THE CHATEAU OF PETIT TRIANON

Taking a deeper liking to Trianon and wishing to enjoy longer stays, Louis XV bade his architect Gabriel build a new pavilion. It was to be a larger construction, situated between the French Garden and the Botanical Garden. Work having commenced in 1763, the finishing touches were added in 1768.

The actual building is cubic; the subfoundation visible only on two sides. It has a main floor over which the attic is surmounted by a balustrade. The skill with which Gabriel varied the four facades, the blending together of proportions, and the refinement of the decorative sculpture make the château a true gem of French neo-classic architecture.

It was here that Louis XV had the first fit of what was to carry him off on May 10, 1774. Given to Marie-Antoinette by Louis XVI, it became the favourite abode of the Queen who would come as often as she could to flee the rigidities of etiquette and to recapture the simple and homely existence she had led in Vienna as a child.

The Cour d'Honneur (Quadrangle) to which we come after walking around the Château is flanked to the left by the Chapel and out buildings. The simplicity of the staircase is enhanced by the handsome gilt wrought iron bannisters and the dazzling lamp of gilded bronze and blue steel. This lamp may well have come from the Château de Bellevue, the residence of the aunts of Louis XVI.

The first Antechamber once had a couple of earthenware stoves which formed a frame to the door leading to the Dining Room. The overdoor is decorated by Carême and Natoire. There are also busts of Louis XVI and the Emperor Joseph II, the Queen's brother.

THE DINING ROOM

We are reminded of the use of this room by the fruit motives on the woodwork and fire-place as well as the themes depicted on the paintings. "Fishing" by Doyen, "The Chase" by Vien, "Wine Harvesting" by Hallé, "The Harvest" by Lagrenée.

THE DINING-ROOM ▲

THE QUEEN'S BEDROOM ▼

The overdoors represent “Boreus and Orythea,” “Flora and Zephyr” by Monnet, “Venus and Adonis” by Belle, also by the same hand “Vertumnus and Pomona.”

Louis XV, according to the fashion of the day, had ordered “disappearing” tables which could be lowered down into the floor boards, but this failed to materialize. Marie-Antoinette turned the Dining Room of Louis XV into a *BILLIARD ROOM.* We can see a commode and a console made by Riesener for the Small Trianon.

THE COMPANY SALON

The decoration of the woodwork is essentially a motive of flowers, the paintings of the overdoors depict the “Metamorphoses” of Ovid. The fine inlaid table was made by Riesener, the pianoforte by Taskin.

Marie-Antoinette, doing away with all protocol, introduced to Trianon the refinements of society life. Here in her time the Royal Family got together, she entertained her guests to the rhythm of the main distractions of the day, music and society games.

THE QUEEN'S BEDCHAMBER

Originally the Private Cabinet of Louis XV, whose Bedroom was situated on the above floor, Queen Marie-Antoinette transformed it into her own Bedchamber. It was decorated with superb furniture “aux épis” (spiked ears of corn), some of which has come down to us: the screen and chairs painted in natural colours and delicately carved, upholstered and embroidered with a motive of wild flowers.

From the door at the back of this room one can see the beautiful *BOUDOIR* with delicate woodwork by Mique. A most clever system of “moving mirrors” was used to cover up the windows at dusk.

We exit by the Cabinet de Toilette (Dressing Room), once the Botanical Library of Louis XV, and where we see a dressing table from the apartment of Marie-Antoinette at the Tuileries.

The little staircase leads up to the attic where Louis XV had his apartment and where, in the course of time, resided Louis XVI, the Dauphin, Madame Royale and Madame Elisabeth.

THE LANDSCAPE GARDEN (jardin paysager)

This English style was designed by Mique on the site of Louis XV's Botanical Garden. The King's plants were sent to the King's Garden in Paris (today Jardin des Plantes). The Queen's architect kept the beautifull trees of different species that Louis XV had had planted and created a landscape of woods and meadows with two ponds and a stream. With the addition of a few workshops this “ensemble” has a trive preromantic air.

THE TEMPLE OF LOVE

This delicate white edifice was built in 1778. The dome is upheld by twelve Corinthian columns and its sculpted decoration by Deschamps represents the emblems of love. This Temple shelters an ancient replica of “Cupid Carving out His Bow From the Club of Hercules” by Bouchardon.

A walk around the Château leads us past a lawn where the Queen had a Chinese merry-go-round set up with mounts of dragons and peacocks.

THE TEMPLE OF LOVE ▲

THE BELVEDERE ▼

A path leads on to *THE QUEEN'S THEATRE* which was built by Mique in 1780. It has an Ionic porch adorned with Cupid sculpted by Deschamps. The Auditorium which is decorated with a most exquisite taste can only seat one hundred people: the Queen, besides the Royal Family, only admitted her own acquaintances and the odd servant. On the other hand, the stage is large enough for the performing of operas: Marie-Antoinette appeared herself on stage, notably in the "Village Deviner" of Jean-Jacques Rousseau and in Beaumarchais "Barber of Seville."

THE BELVEDERE

This delightful octogonal pavilion, where the Queen would rest and enjoy light meals, overlooks the pond. The bas-reliefs on the windows symbolize the seasons while the ornamental front of the doors are decorated with the attributes of the chase and gardening. There is a beautiful marble mosaic on the floor and the stucco bedecked walls are decorated with fine arabesques by Le Riche.

Behind the Belvedere there is a hidden grotto and, not far away, we can see the Orangery and the House of Richard, the Gardener of Louis XV.

THE QUEEN'S HAMLET

By following the brook we soon reach the Hamlet; its twelve thatched roofed houses were built by Mique in 1783. Far from being a theatrical setting as was so often the case for Hamlets built at that period, the Queen's Hamlet was a real farm and its product was served at her table.

We first comme to the *DAIRY OF CLEANLINESS* where milk coming from the *PREPARATION DAIRY* was stored in jars upon marble shelves. The latter was not far away but no longer stands today. *THE MALBOROUGHT TOWER* overlooks the pond, and the *FISHERY* used to be in its basement.

THE BARN, which could also be used as a ballroom, no longer exists. Somewhat further away the *FARM* buildings can be seen. After passing the *MALL* we come across *THE GUARDS' HOUSE, THE DOVECOT* and finally *THE QUEEN'S HOUSE,* beyond which stand *THE HEATING-HOUSE, THE BOUDOIR* and lastly *THE WATER MILL.*

T[illegible] QUEEN'S HOUSE

This construction, which is the biggest of the Hamlet, is in fact made up of two distinct buildings connected by a wooden gallery, ornamented with blue and white earthenware flowerpots with the Queen's initials. The Billiard House on the left has a Billiard Room on the ground-floor and upstairs a small apartment made up of two rooms, a library and two small rooms. The Queen's House has, on the right ground floor, a dining and a backgammon room and upstairs a Chinese room as well as a large and a small salon.

Marie-Antoinette, always very simply dressed in a white muslin dress and straw hat, could watch the field work of the inhabitants from the gallery and momentarily forget the cares of the Queen of France.

THE QUEEN'S HOUSE

LES ÉDITIONS D'ART

11, Rue Colbert
78000 VERSAILLES

Imprimé en France
FIF 91740 Pussay